MAR   2007

043862995

Easy-to-Do Card Tricks for Children

by Karl Fulves

Illustrated by Joseph K. Schmidt

DOVER PUBLICATIONS, INC., New York

Easy-to-Do Card Tricks for Children is a new work, first published by Dover Publications, Inc., in 1989.

Manufactured in the United States of America
Dover Publications, Inc., 31 East 2nd Street, Mineola, N.Y. 11501

Library of Congress Cataloging-in-Publication Data

Fulves, Karl.
  Easy-to-do card tricks for children / by Karl Fulves.
      p.   cm.
  Summary: Instructions and diagrams take aspiring magicians through thirty card tricks, arranged in increasing order of difficulty.
    ISBN 0-486-26153-0
    1. Card tricks—Juvenile literature. [1. Card tricks. 2. Magic tricks.] I. Title.
GV1549.F82   1989
  795.4'38—dc20   89-35382
                                                                        CIP
                                                                        AC

Introduction ♣

Card magic is the most popular branch of magic. Card tricks can be performed almost anywhere and are always well received.

The person starting out in magic should have a choice of tricks that are easy to learn, yet strong enough to amuse and entertain audiences. The tricks in this book are just such a collection. They can be learned by the beginner who has no special skill with cards.

The tricks have been arranged so the simplest are at the beginning of the book. Those requiring more handling are in the later pages. As the reader gains confidence with the early material, he or she can go on to master the tricks that call for more attention to detail.

Of the many observations made about magic, three are fundamental. First, practice each trick so you can perform it without having to stop and think about which step comes next. Second, never repeat a trick for the same audience; someone who asks you to do a trick again is really saying he was fooled the first time. Third, never reveal how a trick is done. People are fascinated with magic tricks and like to be fooled. Keeping the secrets to yourself is the best way to guarantee your audiences will stay fooled.

Most of the tricks in this book can be done any time with any regular deck of cards. A few of the tricks require preparation. It is a good idea to perform two tricks together so that if you do one trick using a prepared deck, you can immediately follow it with a trick that requires no preparation.

"Patter" is the name given by magicians to the talk delivered during a trick. Patter ideas are suggested for the tricks in this book, but you are encouraged to develop a topical line of patter. Good sources of patter material include popular television shows and movies, comics and newscasts.

The tricks in the following pages cover a variety of effects, from rising cards and gambling tricks to mind reading and card locations. Pick tricks from different categories, never do more than two or three card tricks at one performance, and you will leave your audience entertained and mystified.

The material in this book is drawn from ideas of Charles Jordan, Alex Elmsley, Bob Hummer and others. For their generous assistance in the preparation of this book I would like to thank Howard Wurst, Neal Thomas, Sam Schwartz and Joseph K. Schmidt.

KARL FULVES

Contents ♠

Easy-to-Do Card Tricks
for Children

The magician takes it easy in this trick. The spectator chooses a card, returns it to the deck and mixes the cards. Without ever touching the pack, the magician reveals the chosen card.

Method: Ask the spectator to remove eight cards from the top of the deck. Tell him to mix the eight cards and choose one.

After the spectator notes the chosen card, he replaces it on top of the deck. Then he places the remainder of the eight-card packet on the deck. At this point the chosen card is eighth from the top of the deck.

Have him cut off about a third of the deck. The exact number of cards is not important as long as the packet contains more than ten cards.

The spectator holds the cut-off packet in his hand. With his other hand he places the top card of the packet under the packet. Then he places the next card on the table.

He places the next card under the packet. Then he places the next card on top of the card that is on the table. He continues this way, dealing under–down–under–down, until all of the cards have been dealt down onto the heap on the table.

Ask him to spread the packet face up on the table. When you look at the faces of the cards, note the card that lies fourth from the face. It is shown by the arrow in the example of Figure 1. This is the chosen card.

Do not reveal it yet. Close your eyes, pretend to receive mystic vibrations from the deck, then reveal the color, suit and value of the chosen card. In the example of Figure 1 you would say, "Your card is red, a heart. Yes, I can see it clearly, the eight of hearts."

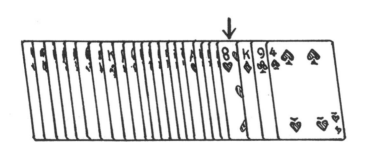

Fig. 1

♠ Infallible

Prediction tricks hint that the magician can see the future. To demonstrate this, the spectator mixes face-up and face-down cards together. Then he divides the cards into two heaps. Each heap contains some face-up cards and some face-down cards.

Taking one heap behind his back, the magician makes an adjustment so that the number of face-up cards in his heap correctly predicts the number of face-up cards in the spectator's heap.

Method: Remove any 20 cards from the deck. Place ten cards face down on the table. Turn the other ten cards face up. Mix the groups together. Make sure face-up cards and face-down cards are well mixed.

Hand the 20-card packet to the spectator. Ask him to mix the cards further. Make sure the spectator does not turn any cards over when he mixes them.

Have him deal ten cards off the top into a heap on the table. Turn your back while he does this. Take the remaining ten cards from him.

Place your ten-card packet under the table or behind the back. Say that you will try to predict the number of face-up cards the spectator has in his packet. With your cards out of sight, turn the packet over. Then bring it into view and place it on the table.

Have the spectator count the number of face-up cards in his packet. He might find six face-up cards. Then have him count the number of face-up cards in your packet. There will also be six face-up cards. You can point out as a bonus that the number of face-down cards also matches.

♣ This Is It!

People are always impressed when you find a card under seemingly impossible conditions. In this routine you produce a card merely thought of by a spectator.

Any 16 cards are used. They are dealt face down into four heaps of four cards each. The cards are dealt one at a time from left to right. The spectator chooses any heap, turns it so he can see the faces and thinks of any one of the four cards.

The magician squares up two of the other heaps and places one on top of the other. Then the heap containing the thought-of card is placed face down on top. The remaining heap is placed on top of all, Figure 2.

Holding the 16-card packet face down, the magician deals the cards into four heaps as follows. The first card is dealt to the upper left, the second card below it, the third card below that and the fourth card below that. The fifth card is dealt on top of the first, the sixth card on top of the second and so on. The dealing sequence is shown by the numbers in Figure 3. All cards are dealt face down.

When all 16 cards have been dealt, turn each heap face up. Be careful not to disturb the order of the cards in each packet when you do so. Spread each packet so the faces of all cards are visible. Ask the spectator which heap contains his card.

When he points to a heap, take note of the second card from the right. In the example shown in Figure 4, that card is the ♥ 5. This is the chosen card. Scoop up the packet, keeping the cards in order. Place the packet face down in the left hand.

Say, "This trick has a name. It's called, 'This is it!' I'll show you why."

Spell, "T-H-I-S," dealing one card for each letter from top to bottom of the packet. Then deal the next card face down onto the table.

Spell, "I-S," dealing one card for each letter from the top to the bottom of the packet. Then deal the next card face down onto the table.

Spell, "I-T," dealing one card for each letter from the top to the bottom of the packet. Deal the next card onto the table.

You will have one card left in your hand. Name the chosen card, that is, the card you noted in Figure 4. In this example you would say, "This is it, the five of hearts!" Turn over the card in hand to show you found the thought-of card.

Fig. 2

Fig. 3

CHOSEN CARD

Fig. 4

♥ Fingerprints

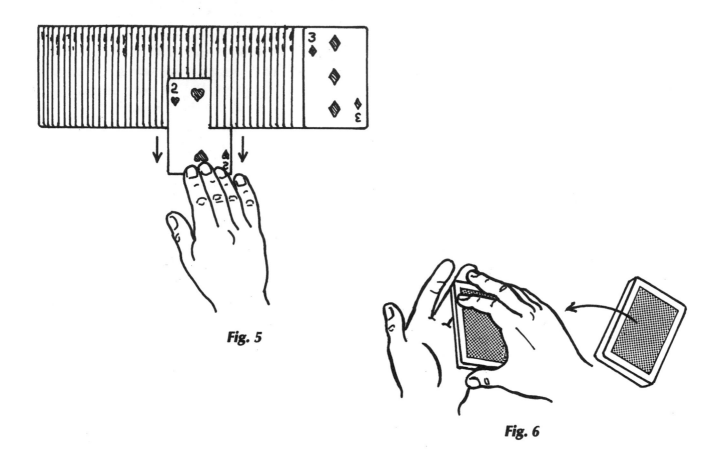

Fig. 5

Fig. 6

Playing the part of a detective, the magician asks a spectator to choose a card and bury it in the deck. Using the spectator's fingerprints, the magician quickly finds the chosen card.

Method: Tell the spectator that you will use the ♥ 2 for this trick. Spread the deck face up on the table and remove the ♥ 2. As you do, note the bottom card of the pack. In Figure 5 the bottom card is the ♦ 3. This will be your key card.

Turn the deck face down and place it before the spectator. Ask him to press his thumb against the face of the ♥ 2 so you will have his thumbprint on file.

After he has done this, ask him to lift off about a third of the deck and place it in his left

hand, Figure 6. Then ask him to lift off another third of the deck and place it on top of the cards in his hand.

While you turn your back or look away, ask him to look at the top card of the packet in his hand. Tell him to press his thumb against the face of this card to leave a thumbprint. Then have him place the chosen card face down on top of the packet in his hand.

To bury his card, have him pick up the lower third of the deck (the portion on the table) and place it on top of the cards in his hand.

Take the deck from him and spread it face up from left to right on the table. Silently note the card to the right of the key card. In Figure 7 this is the ♠ 10. The ♠ 10 is the chosen card. Remember this card.

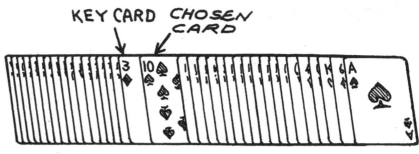

KEY CARD CHOSEN CARD

Spread cards about the table. Glance at the face of the two of hearts from time to time, as if comparing the spectator's thumbprint with prints you have spotted on other cards. Then pretend to notice the ♠10 for the first time. Compare it to the ♥ 2. Say, "The prints match. You must have chosen the ten of spades."

Fig. 7

The Gambler ♦

Gambling tricks always hold the audience's attention. After the spectator cuts the deck, the magician deals out two poker hands. The magician shows he got the winning hand; he dealt himself the four kings.

Method: Beforehand, place any four of a kind on top of the deck. We will use kings in this example. When ready to perform, place the deck on the table. Ask the spectator to cut off about half the pack. As he does, say, "I saw a show on television where a fellow dealt the winning hand. Let's see if I remember how he did it."

Have the spectator deal the cut-off portion into five heaps. He does this by dealing a card at a time from left to right. He continues dealing until he runs out of cards. Pick up the first packet by grasping it at the sides. Draw the top and bottom card off together as shown in Figure 8. Place the pair of cards together on the table. Put the remainder of the packet on top of the deck.

Pick up the next packet. Draw off the top

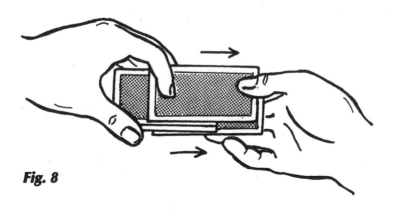

Fig. 8

and bottom card together as before. Place this pair on top of the first pair. Put the remainder of the packet on top of the deck.

Perform the same actions with each of the other two packets. When you finish, you will have a packet of ten cards on the table.

Deal out two poker hands by dealing a card to the spectator, one to yourself, one to the spectator, one to yourself, and so on until all ten cards have been dealt.

Turn up the spectator's hand. Say, "This is the way it looked on T.V. You got the start of a pretty good hand. The dealer gave himself a hand that was even better."

Turn up your hand to show the four kings.

♠ Nerve

A shuffled deck is placed on the table. The magician reads the spectator's mind before he chooses a card. Then the spectator chooses a card. Immediately the magician names the card. Throughout the trick it appears as if the magician never touched the deck.

Method: This trick requires more nerve than anything else. It should be performed before one spectator. If any others are present they will catch on to the secret.

Have a spectator shuffle the deck and place it on the table. He can use his own cards.

Stand facing him. Place the first finger of each hand on the spectator's forehead, Figure 9. The fingers should be about an inch apart. Remark that you want to take a reading of the spectator's thought waves.

Say that you are picking up too much static. Take your hands away. Say it would be better if the spectator closed his eyes. When he does so, pretend to place your first fingers back on his forehead. Actually, you place the first and second fingers of the right hand there, Figure 10. To the spectator the situation will feel the same as in Figure 9.

Quickly and quietly spot the top card of the deck as shown in Figure 10. Then bring the hands to the sides and have the spectator open his eyes.

Ask him to note the top card of the deck. Tell him to remember the card, place it on top of the deck and give the deck a cut to bury the card. Touch your fingertips to his forehead and announce the name of the chosen card.

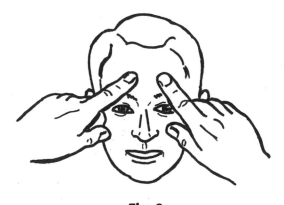

Fig. 9

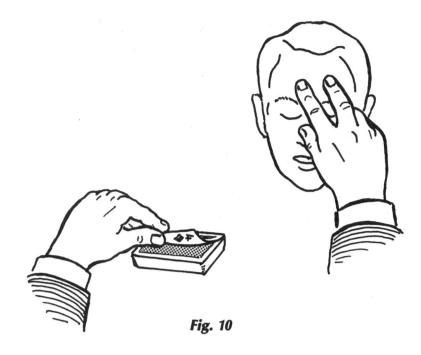

Fig. 10

Bermuda Triangle ♦

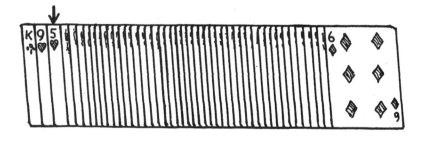

Fig. 11

In this trick the magician evokes the mystery of the Bermuda Triangle to find a chosen card. The Bermuda Triangle is an area of the Atlantic Ocean where mysterious forces are said to exist.

Method: Have the spectator shuffle and cut the deck. Spread the deck on the table to show the audience that the cards are well mixed. As you do, remember the card third from the top. In Figure 11 this card is the ♥ 5.

Scoop up the deck and place it face down on the table. Ask the spectator to cut it into three piles. Keep track of which pile is the top portion of the deck. Arrange the three piles in the shape of a triangle, Figure 12, *A* being the top portion of the deck.

Say, "This trick uses the mystery of the

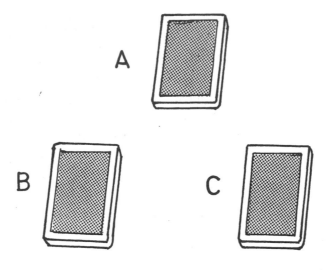

Fig. 12

Bermuda Triangle. That's why the cards are placed in the shape of a triangle. We need to adjust the cards a little." Place a card from B onto C. Place a card from A onto B. Study the cards as if they are not quite right. Place two cards from C onto B. Then place one card from A onto C.

Say, "I can feel the power of the triangle." Point to A and have the spectator look at the top card. Ask him to concentrate on the card.

Place one hand on B and the other hand on C. Close your eyes. Say, "The three corners of the mental triangle are the color, suit and value of your card." The chosen card is the one you noted in Figure 11. Since it is the ♥ 5 in this example, you would say, "I see red, heart, five. You must have chosen the five of hearts."

♣ Antigravity

The magician causes a card to rise mysteriously from the deck. There are no gimmicks. Any deck may be used.

Method: Have a card chosen and placed on top of the deck. Hold the deck in the hand so the thumb is at one long edge and the fingers at the other. The correct grip is shown in Figure 13.

Extend the first finger of the right hand. Place it on the top edge of the deck. Slide the finger back and forth along the top edge of the cards. Say that this generates heat. Bring the first finger to rest at about the center of the top edge.

Secretly extend the little finger so it touches the back of the top card. The situation is shown in Figure 14. The audience cannot see the extended little finger because it is hidden by the deck.

Say, "When I rub the cards, it produces heat, and we all know that heat rises." Slowly move the right hand up about an inch. Because the little finger is in contact with the top card of the deck, the top card will slide upward as shown in Figure 14. From the audience's view, the top card seems to rise mysteriously from the deck.

When the card has risen about an inch, curl the little finger in toward the palm. Keep the top card in place with the left thumb and fingers. Use the extended first finger to push the top card flush with the deck again.

The trick can also be done as follows. Hold the deck as in Figure 13. Then drape a handkerchief over the deck, but be sure to leave a portion of the top card exposed as shown by the arrow in Figure 15.

Place the extended forefinger on top of the deck. Then extend the little finger so it touches the top card at the position shown by the arrow in Figure 15. Proceed from here with the handling as described above. The presence of the handkerchief seems to isolate the deck from the hand, making the trick that much more puzzling.

Fig. 13

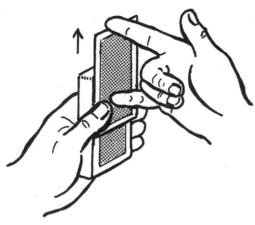

Fig. 14

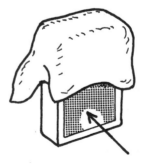

Fig. 15

♣ The Magic Spell

Using the ♦ A through ♦ 7, the magician spells out the cards in order. The spectator will find it difficult or impossible to duplicate the feat.

Method: Arrange the ♦ A through ♦ 7 as shown in Figure 16, with the ♦ 2 on top of the packet, the ♦ 3 next, and so on to the ♦ 7 at the bottom.

Hold the packet face down in the left hand. Say to the audience, "Once I took a spelling test. This is how it turned out."

Spell "A–C–E" out loud. As you do, transfer a card from the top of the packet to the bottom for each letter. When you finish, say "Ace" and turn up the top card of the packet. It will be the ace. Place the ace face up on the table.

Spell "T–W–O" out loud, dealing one card at a time, one for each letter, from the top of the packet, to the bottom. When you finish, say "Two" and turn up the next card to reveal the two. Place the two on the table.

In the same way spell each of the remaining cards ("THREE," "FOUR," "FIVE," "SIX"). In each case deal a card from top to bottom for each letter you spell, turn up the next card and reveal the card you just spelled.

After spelling the ace through six, you will have one card remaining in the hand. Say, "And that leaves the seven." Turn up the last card to show the seven.

Say to the spectators, "Would you care to try it?" If they do not know the setup, the spectators will find it difficult to duplicate the feat.

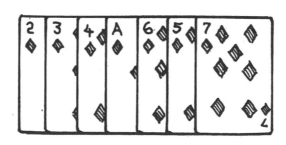

Fig. 16

Love Match ♠

This is an unusual trick in which two picture cards change the way they look at one another. The ♣Q and ♠J are fastened together with paper clips, Figure 17. Another card is placed against them, Figure 18. The magician explains that the queen and jack had a lovers' quarrel and were not seeing eye to eye. As shown in Figure 18, the queen faces one way, the jack the opposite way.

The cards are covered a moment. When they are next shown, the jack and queen have patched things up. Now they are gazing into each other's eyes, Figure 19.

Method: Remove the ♣Q and the ♠J from the deck. Fasten them together with paper clips as shown in Figure 17. Place another card face down on top of them in the position shown in Figure 18. In this example, the third card is the ♥7. The jack and queen should be facing away from one another. If not, turn them around end for end and place the face-down card against them.

Turn the three cards around side for side so they face the audience. The magician's view is shown in Figure 20. Point out that the

Fig. 17

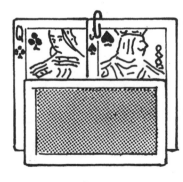

Fig. 18

Fig. 19

jack and queen had a lovers' quarrel and were not seeing eye to eye.

Place the three cards behind the back or under the table. When they are concealed from the spectator's view, turn them around end for end, Figure 21. Then slide the third card (the ♥ 7 in our example) downward to the position shown in Figure 22.

Hold up the three cards so the audience can see them. Point out that the jack and queen have made up. Now they face one another.

In some decks the ♣ Q and ♠ J have a different design and will not face properly to perform the trick. In this case you can usually find other picture cards in the deck that will work just as well.

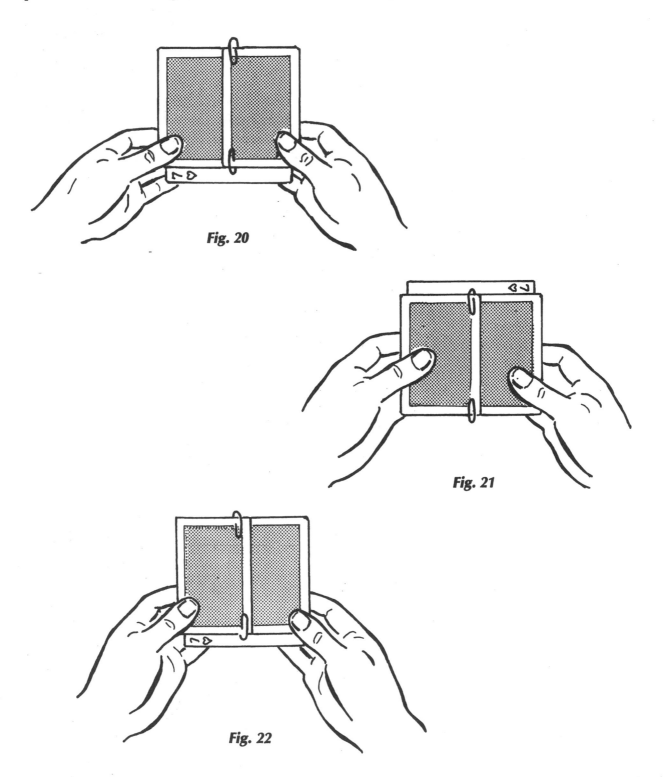

Fig. 20

Fig. 21

Fig. 22

Novelty tricks are a good change of pace. In this amusing routine the spectator cuts off a packet of cards and deals the packet into three heaps. He places the top card of each heap in his pocket. Using the X-ray vision of the ♦ J, the magician reveals the value of each hidden card. Any borrowed deck may be used for this trick.

Method: When the borrowed deck is handed to you, hold the cards so you can see the faces. As you spread the cards looking for the ♦ J, remember the values of the three cards at the bottom (or face) of the deck. In Figure 23 these cards are a 2, 9 and 5. Just remember them as 295.

Remove the ♦ J. Say, "Normally, the jack has 20/20 vision." As you speak, tap the jack into a glass, Figure 24. Say, "With glasses, he gains X-ray vision."

Place the deck face down on the table. Have the spectator cut off half and place the cut-off upper portion aside. He then deals the lower half into three packets. Ask him to place the top card of each packet into his pocket.

Point the glass at the spectator's pocket. Then hold the glass to your ear as if listening to a telephone message. Slowly recite the values of the cards you memorized. In our example you would say, "The jack says he saw a two, a nine and a five in your pocket." The spectator removes the three cards and verifies that the jack has perfect vision.

With practice you can memorize the value and suit of each of the bottom three cards. Then you can reveal the complete identity of each of the three cards.

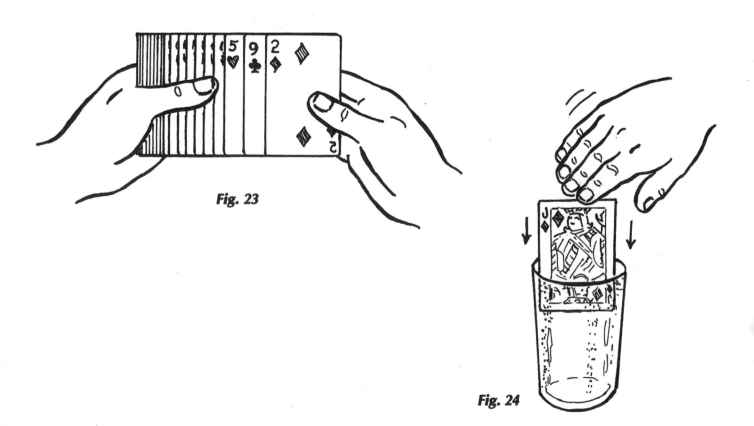

Fig. 23

Fig. 24

♣ Mind Over Matter

Audiences are always impressed by tricks in which the magician seems to read the spectator's mind. This is one such card routine. The magician reveals a card only thought of by the spectator.

Method: Deal out five packets of five cards each. Take the cards one at a time from the top of the deck, dealing from left to right. When you have dealt out 25 cards, place the rest of the deck aside.

Ask a spectator to choose one packet, mix the cards and remember any card in the packet. Have him mix the cards once more. Then he replaces the packet on the table.

Pick up any packet that does not contain his card. Drop it onto any other packet that does not contain his card. Drop this combined heap on top of the packet that contains his card. Place this heap on top of one of the remaining packets. Finally place the heap on top of the one remaining packet.

Deal out five packets of five cards each. Deal as before by taking the cards one at a time off the top and dealing from left to right.

When you have dealt out all 25 cards, ask the spectator to find the packet that contains his thought-of card. Make sure the order of the cards in each packet is maintained. Take the packet from him and spread it so you can see the faces.

Remove the center card of the packet (that is, the card that lies third from the top). Place it face down on the table. Ask him to name his card. Then have him turn over the card on the table to reveal you found the correct card.

♦ The Message Deck

Card tricks should entertain as well as baffle the audience. In this routine the cards act as if programmed like a computer.

The magician places a message in the deck. A freely chosen card is found by a process of elimination. It turns out the message correctly predicts when the card would be found.

Method: Tear a piece of paper so it is a little smaller than a playing card. On one side write "Stop!" On the other side write "The last card!" Place the paper in your pocket until you are ready to perform.

To do the trick, count 26 cards off the top of the deck. Place the paper on the lower packet so you can see the word "Stop!" and place the upper packet back on top, Figure 25.

Say, "This deck is programmed to find a card." Deal 16 cards off the top of the deck. Let the spectator mix the 16-card packet and choose one card. Ask him to place the chosen card on top of the lower portion of the deck (that is, on top of the packet that contains the message). Then place the 15-card packet on top of all.

Say, "The deck is programmed in an odd

way. It doesn't know what card you chose but it *does* know what cards you *didn't* choose."

Push cards off the top of the deck without disturbing their order until you come to the message. Point to the word "Stop!" and say, "This tells me when to stop." You now hold a packet of 26 cards in the hand. The sixteenth card from the top is the spectator's card.

Deal the first card off the top, turn it face up and place it on the table. Deal the next card face down into a separate heap near yourself. Deal the next card face up onto the face-up card. Figure 26 shows the situation at this point. Deal the next card face down onto the face-down card.

Continue dealing this way, dealing every other card face up onto the face-up heap until you have dealt all 26 cards. You will have one face-up heap and one face-down heap. Say,

"The deck knows you didn't pick one of the face-up cards." Pick up the face-up heap and place it aside.

Pick up the other heap of 13 face-down cards. Deal this into two heaps in the same way by dealing the first card onto a face-up heap, the next onto a face-down heap, and so on, dealing every other card face up as before. Once again the spectator's card will not show up in the face-up heap. Place this heap aside.

Again deal into two heaps, discarding the face-up heap. Continue the process until you are left with just one card. Ask the spectator to name his card. When he does, turn over the last card to show it is the one he chose.

Say, "The deck always knows your card will be last." Turn over the piece of paper to reveal the words "The last card!"

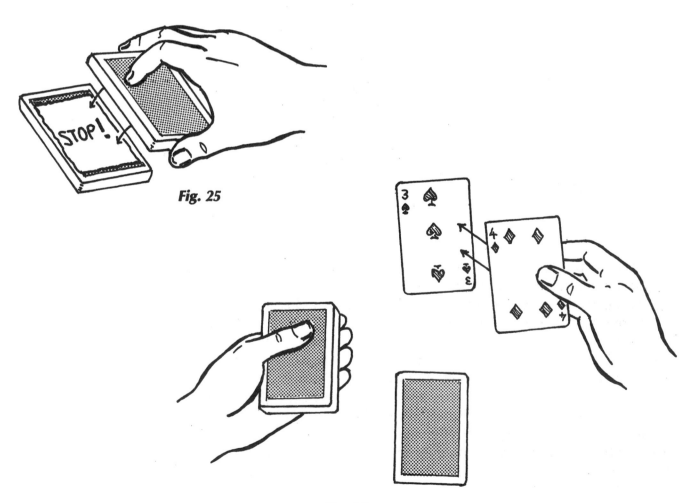

Fig. 25

Fig. 26

♠ Gambler's Dream

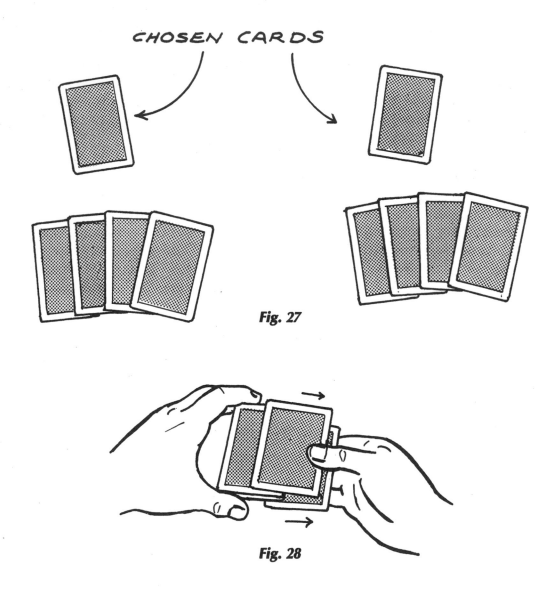

CHOSEN CARDS

Fig. 27

Fig. 28

In this routine, the magician shows how the gambler stacks the deck. In the process, two chosen cards are found in a surprising way. Any deck may be used.

Method: Remove five black cards and place them face down in a heap in front of the spectator. Remove five red cards and place them face down in a heap in front of yourself.

You and the spectator each choose a card from your respective packets. The chosen cards are placed face down on the table. The situation is shown in Figure 27. Each person

can initial the face of his card to make sure he remembers it.

Place your packet on top of the spectator's. Place the spectator's chosen card on top of the packet. Then drop the packet on top of your chosen card. At this point, the spectator's card is on top of the packet and your card is on the bottom.

Hold the packet by the ends with the left hand. Draw off the top and bottom cards together with the right hand, Figure 28. Place this pair of cards on the table.

Draw off the next pair of cards in the same

way (one from the top and one from the bottom). Place this pair of cards on top of the first pair.

Continue drawing off pairs of cards the same way, placing each pair on top of those on the table, until all five pairs have been dealt. As you do this, say, "That's how the gambler stacks the cards."

Place the packet face down in the left hand. Deal out two hands of poker by dealing a card off the top to the spectator, the next card to yourself, the next card to the spectator, the next to yourself, and so on until all ten cards have been dealt.

Say, "All my cards are black except the red card I chose." Turn up your packet to show four blacks plus the chosen red card.

"And all your cards are red except the black card you chose." Turn up his poker hand to show all red cards except the chosen black card. Say, "No wonder some gamblers win all the time!"

A Fortune ♥

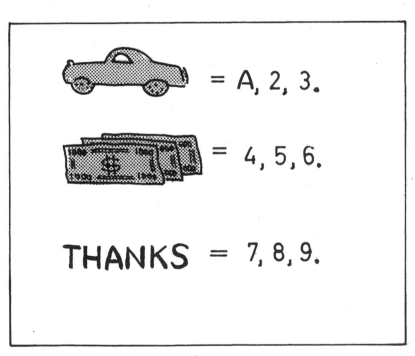

Fig. 29

This is a simple way for a lucky person to win a big prize. The magician shows the chart shown in Figure 29. He explains that if the spectator chooses an ace, two or three, he wins a new toy car. If he chooses four, five or six, he wins a million dollars in play money. On the other hand, if he chooses seven, eight or nine, he wins an expression of thanks from the magician.

The spectator chooses a card from his own deck and wins (what else?) the piece of paper expressing the magician's thanks.

Method: When the borrowed deck is handed to you, cut any 7, 8 or 9 to the top. The way to do this is as follows. Say you spot the ♠ 7 in the middle of the pack. Cut the deck and complete the cut so the ♠ 7 is now on top.

Count 26 cards off the top into a heap on the table. Count the cards one at a time off the top. Make sure you count carefully so you have exactly 26 cards. Then pick up the counted heap and place it on top of the deck. The ♠ 7 is now twenty-sixth from the top of the deck.

On a piece of paper jot down the chart shown in Figure 29. Place the deck on the table. Ask the spectator to cut off about a quarter of the deck. The number of cards he takes is not important as long as he cuts off less than half the deck.

When he has cut off a packet, pick up the remainder of the deck and count 25 cards off the top, one at a time, onto a heap on the table. Place the rest of the deck aside.

Ask him to count the number of cards he cut. Say he cut 14 cards. Have him count to the fourteenth card in the 25-card heap. It will be the ♠ 7.

He then consults the chart to discover that all he has won is your thanks. Gently tell him, "Better luck next time."

◆ Lucky Seven

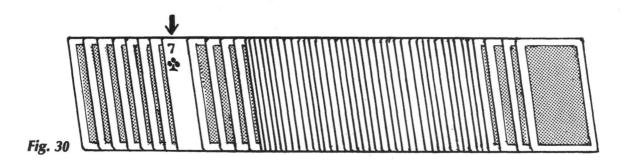

Fig. 30

The spectator chooses a card and returns it to the pack. The magician causes a card to turn face up in the pack mysteriously. This card is a seven-spot. He counts seven cards off and turns up the chosen card.

Method: Before you perform the trick, place a reversed seven-spot eighth from the bottom of the deck, Figure 30. An easy way to do this is to remove the ♣ 7 and place it aside. Deal seven cards face down off the top of the deck onto a heap on the table. Place the ♣ 7 face up on top of the heap. Then place the rest of the deck face down on top of all. This preparation is done secretly.

Tell the audience, "This is a detective story about a private eye named Sam Seven. He practiced his trade by tracking down chosen cards."

Place the deck face down on the table. Ask the spectator to cut off about half the deck, remove a card and replace the cut packet back on the deck.

He looks at the card he cut to and places it on top of the deck. Then he cuts the deck and completes the cut to bury the chosen card. Say, "No one in the deck claimed to know where the chosen card was. That's why it was called a pack of lies. But Sam did have an informant."

Snap the fingers. Spread the cards between the hands to reveal the reversed seven. Place all the cards above the ♣ 7 on the table. Deal the seven onto the table.

Say, "That seven told Sam he was seven steps away from his man." Count seven cards off the remainder of the deck. Turn up the next card and it will be the chosen card.

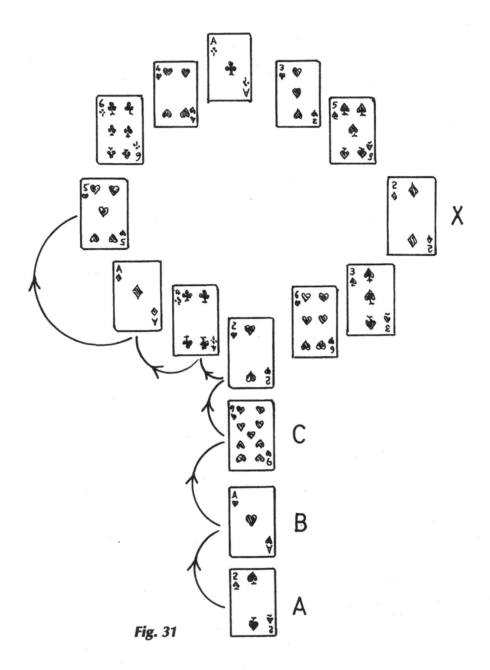

Fig. 31

The psychic known as Dr. Q had no trouble predicting the future. To show the kind of thing he could do, the magician deals cards on the table to form the letter Q. The spectator picks a number and counts that number of cards twice to arrive at a chosen card. In the manner of Dr. Q, the magician correctly predicts which card would be chosen.

Method: You will need a deck of cards, an envelope and a piece of paper. On the address side of the envelope write the words "A PREDICTION." Place the envelope on the table so the address side is down.

Have the spectator shuffle and cut his own deck of cards. Lay out 15 cards face up in the shape of the letter Q as shown in Figure 31.

Fig. 32

Remark that Dr. Q used this layout as his trademark.

Pick up pencil and paper. Secretly note the card that lies in the three-o'clock position on the circular layout. In other words, if you picture the circular layout as a clock face with the tail of the Q at the six-o'clock position, you will predict the card that is at the position marked by the X in Figure 31. Fold the prediction and place it in the envelope.

Turn each card face down in place. The situation at this point is as indicated in Figure 31, only all cards are now face down.

Ask the spectator for a number between five and 15. Place a penny on the card shown as A in Figure 31. Moving the penny from the card labeled A, the spectator counts up to the

left until he has counted the chosen number. If the spectator chose the number six, then he would count six cards from A in the direction of the arrows in Figure 31, ending up at the card in the nine-o'clock position. He places the penny on this card.

Remove the tail of the Q. These are the cards shown as A, B and C in Figure 31. Place them on the deck as you say, "It'll speed things up if we get these out of the way."

From the card where the penny is, the spectator counts the same number of cards in a counterclockwise direction. In our example, the spectator chose the number six. He moves the penny six spaces as shown by the arrow in Figure 32. The penny will now rest on the card at the three-o'clock position.

Have him turn this card over. Say, "Before we started, I wrote a prediction." Hold up the envelope, Figure 33, to show you did indeed write "A PREDICTION" on the envelope. Then open the envelope, have the prediction read and show that it matches the card on which the penny now rests.

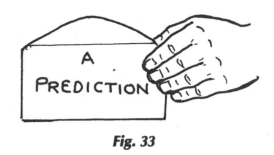

Fig. 33

The Joker Thinks ♥

The day may not be far off when robots will perform card tricks. In this trick a joker is used instead of a robot. It correctly reveals the identity of two chosen cards.

Method: When the borrowed deck is handed to you, hold it so you can see the faces of the cards. Spread the cards as you remark that you will need the joker for this trick (if no joker is present, use the ♠ K). When you look through the deck for the joker, secretly note the top card of the deck. We will assume this card is the ♦ 9.

Remove the joker and openly place it on the bottom of the deck. Then place the deck face down in front of the spectator. Have him grasp a packet of cards from the top of the deck with his left hand, and then another packet with the right hand. He places the two packets on the table as shown in Figure 34. Packet A came from the top of the deck. The ♦ 9 is on top of this packet.

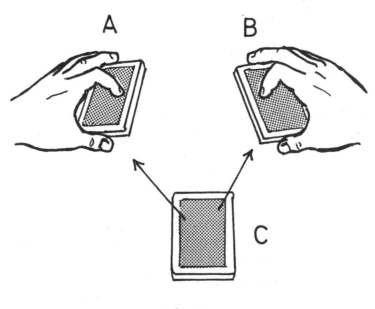

Fig. 34

Fig. 35

Remove the joker from the bottom of packet C and place it face up on top of packet C. Say, "When my assistant isn't available, the joker helps out."

Pick up the top card of packet B. Keep it face down. Hold it over the joker for a moment. Say, "The joker thinks this card is the nine of diamonds." Here you name the card you previously noted as the top card of the deck.

Place the card into your jacket or shirt pocket. As you do, glance at the face of the card, Figure 35. The card is the ♦ 3 in our example. Pick up the top card of packet A. Hold it face down over the joker.

Then say, "He thinks this card is the three of diamonds." Now name the card you glimpsed in Figure 35. Place this card in the same pocket.

Say, "The joker guessed that the cards would be the nine of diamonds and the three of diamonds. Let's see how well he did."

Remove the two cards. Toss them out face up to show the joker was correct in both cases.

♠ Crazy Colors

The spectator shuffles the two halves of the deck together. The deck is cut into three heaps. Instantly it is shown that one heap contains all red cards, and another all black.

Method: Place 13 blacks in a heap on the table. Place 26 reds on top of them, and the remaining 13 blacks on top of all. The assembled deck looks like Figure 36. Place the deck in its case.

When ready to perform, remove the deck from its case. Ask the spectator to count 26 cards off the top, one at a time, into a heap on the table. Then have him riffle shuffle the

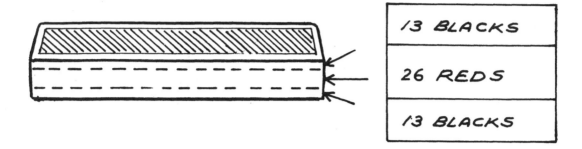

| /3 BLACKS |
| 26 REDS |
| /3 BLACKS |

Fig. 36

two halves of the deck together as shown in Figure 37. Choose a spectator who can riffle the packets together evenly.

Have him square the deck and place it on the table. Ask him to cut off about two-thirds of the deck and place this packet to the right of the bottom third. Then have him cut off about half the larger packet and place this to the right of the other two packets.

Pick up the middle packet, mix the cards and turn them so you can see the faces. Remove a red card and a black card. Put the mixed packet aside.

Wave the red card over the packet that was on top of the deck originally. Say, "Red attracts red." Turn this packet face up and spread it on the table to reveal all red cards.

Wave the black card over the packet that was originally on the bottom of the deck. Say, "Black attracts black." Turn this packet face up. Spread it on the table to show all black cards.

Another trick using colors is "Astral Mind," which is described next. It can be used as a follow-up routine to "Crazy Colors."

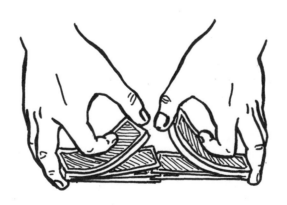

Fig. 37

♦ Astral Mind

Fig. 38

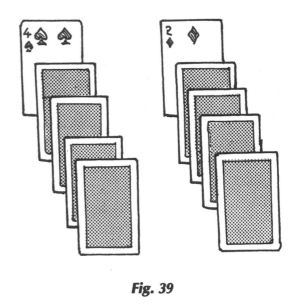

Fig. 39

The magician removes some red cards and some black cards from the deck. The spectator does not know which cards are which color, yet he succeeds in correctly guessing the colors of all cards.

Method: When the borrowed deck is handed to you, hold it with the faces toward you. Make sure no one else can see the faces of the cards. Remove a red card and place it face down on the table. Then remove a black card and place it on top of the red. Next remove a red card and place it on the cards that are on the table. Next remove a black, then a red, and so on, alternating the colors until you have a heap of ten cards on the table. The colors will alternate black–red from top to bottom.

Place the deck aside. Hold the packet of ten cards face down. Withdraw the top card, turn it face up and place it on the table. Withdraw the next card and place it face up a few inches from the first card. The situation will be as shown in Figure 38.

Say that you are going to ask the spectator to guess the colors of the remaining cards

and that the face-up cards (the ♠ 4 and ♦ 2 in Figure 38) will be used to record his guesses.

Place the packet behind the back. Remove the bottom card. Unknown to the audience, this card is red. Hold it face down as you bring it around in front. Ask the spectator if he thinks the card is red. If he says yes, place it face down on the face-up ♦ 2.

If he says no, place it behind the back. Pretend to remove another card from the packet. Bring the same card out in front again. Say, "Do you think *this* card is red?" If he says yes, place it face down on the face-up ♦ 2. If he says no, place it behind the back, pretend to remove another card, then bring the same card out again.

After the spectator has said yes to a red card, place the packet behind the back. Remove the new bottom card. Unknown to the audience, this card is black. Bring the card into view. Say, "Do you think this card is black?" If the spectator answers yes, place it face down on top of the four of spades.

If he says no, bring the card behind the back, pretend to remove another card from the packet, but bring the same card into view again. Make sure to keep all cards face down so the spectators cannot see the faces. Say, "Do you think *this* card is black?" If he says yes, place it face down on top of the ♠ 4. If he says no, return the card behind the back, pretend to take another card, but bring out the same card.

Continue in this way until you have one card left. Toss this face-down card onto the ♠ 4. At the finish the situation will appear as in Figure 39. Remind the spectator that he had a free choice on every card.

Turn over the cards on the face-up black card to show he guessed correctly on all the blacks. Turn over the other four cards to show he guessed correctly on all the reds.

Flyaway ♣

Fig. 40

Fig. 41

Fig. 42

In this baffling trick the spectator shuffles the deck and removes six cards. The names of these cards are jotted down on a piece of paper. The magician crosses out one card, say the ♥ 3, from the list. Immediately the ♥ 3 vanishes from the deck. It is found inside the card case.

Method: Before the performance, put one card into the card case. In Figure 40 this card is the ♥ 3. Tuck the flap into the card case on top of the ♥ 3 as shown in Figure 41. Then slide the rest of the deck into the case, Figure 42. This completes the preparation.

When performing the trick, remove the deck from the case and hand it out to be shuffled. Unknown to the audience, the ♥ 3 is still inside the card case.

When the deck has been shuffled, have the spectator deal off the top six cards. Hand him pencil and paper. As you read off the names of the six cards, ask him to jot them down on the paper.

Hold the six cards so you alone can see the faces. Name the first four cards correctly. When you get to the fifth card, name the ♥ 3 (that is, name the card hidden inside the card case). Name the sixth card correctly.

Place the six cards on top of the deck, cut the deck and complete the cut. Then give the deck a quick shuffle to mix the cards.

Take the list from the spectator. Say, "I'm going to pick one card from the list and try to make it disappear." Cross out the ♥ 3. Snap the fingers over the deck and say, "The three of hearts has vanished."

Let the spectator examine the deck to verify that the ♥ 3 is no longer in the deck. When he has done this, pick up the card case. Pull out the flap, then tap the card case against the deck. Turn the card case over so the ♥ 3 falls out onto the table.

♠ The Secret

The spectator takes any 12 cards from the deck and mixes them. He notes a card and its position in the packet. Then he alters the position of the chosen card. Although the magician does not know the card or its position, he is able to restore the card to its original position in the packet.

Method: Let the spectator take any 12 cards from the deck and mix them. While you turn your back, he writes a number from one to six on a piece of paper. Then he notes the card at that position from the top of the packet.

For example, he might write the number three. The third card might be the ♣ 7. Ask the spectator to write the name of the card on the paper. Then he hides the paper.

Whatever the position of the card, ask him to transfer that many cards one at a time from the bottom to the top of the packet. Turn your head aside while he does this so

you cannot see how many cards he transfers.

Take the packet. Say, "The problem is to put your card back in its original position, even though I don't know your card."

Hold the packet face down in the hand. Deal cards off the top, one at a time, to form two heaps. The first card is dealt to the left, the next card to the right, the next to the left, the next to the right, and so on until all 12 cards have been dealt.

Place the left-hand heap on top of the right-hand heap. Say, "I want to check that I've got it right." Deal the packet into a face-down heap by dealing the cards off the top, one at a time, until all 12 cards have been dealt.

Ask the spectator for the original position of his card. In this example he will say his card was third from the top. He counts to the third card and discovers that his card is indeed back in its original position.

Surprise Reverse ♥

In this trick the spectator chooses a card and returns it to the deck. The magician does not know the card, yet he makes it reverse itself in the pack.

Method: Use any borrowed deck. Spread the cards face down between the hands and have the spectator choose a card. While he looks at the card, say that you want to mix the cards behind your back.

When you place the pack behind the back, turn it over so it is face up. Turn the face card over so it is face down. Put it back on the face of the deck as shown in Figure 43.

Keep the deck squared and bring it into view. Have the spectator return his card face down to the pack as shown in Figure 44. The deck appears to be face down but really it is

only the face card that is face down. The rest of the deck is face up. Be careful not to spread the cards when the spectator returns his card to the deck.

Place the deck behind your back. Say you will try to find the card in less than three seconds. When the pack is out of sight, turn the face down card over and replace it on the face of the deck.

Turn the deck over so it is face down. Bring the deck into view. Say, "I found your card and put it back in the deck in less than three seconds." The audience may not believe you, so you add, "Of course I put it back reversed."

Spread the deck face down on the table. The spectator's card will be face up in the middle of the pack as shown in Figure 45.

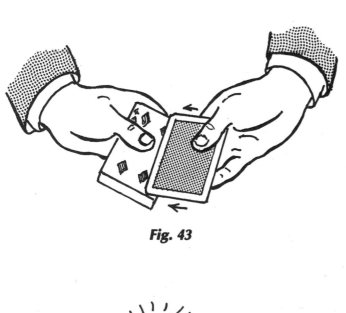

Fig. 43

Fig. 44

Fig. 45

♦ Magnetic Fingers

The spectator chooses one of four cards. Each card is placed under one of the spectator's fingers. The spectator can lift each finger freely, but due to a mysterious magnetic effect, he cannot lift the finger that contacts the chosen card.

Method: Remove any four cards from the deck. Let the spectator choose one, show it to the others and place it face down on the table. Drop the other three cards face down on top of it.

State that you will mix the cards. Take the top card off the packet and place it under the packet. Take the next card and put it face down on the table. Place the next card under the packet, and the next on top of the card of the table. Place the next card under the packet and the next card on top of the packet on the table. Place the last card on top of the packet on the table.

Ask the spectator to place his right hand palm down on the table with the fingers outstretched. Then have him curl the second (middle) finger in under the palm. Slip the top card of the packet under his thumb, the next card under his first (index) finger, the next card under his third finger and the final card under his little finger. The situation is shown in Figure 46.

Remark that there is a magnetic force between his card and his hand. Tap the spectator's thumb. Say, "Lift your thumb." The spectator has no trouble doing this.

Tap his first finger. Say, "Lift this finger." He has no trouble doing so.

Now tap his third finger. Say, "Lift this finger." He will find it difficult or impossible to lift this finger. Say, "The force is keeping you from lifting your finger. What card did you choose?"

When he names the card, slide the card out from under his third finger. Turn it over to show it is the chosen card.

Fig. 46

Easy Aces ♣

In this trick the spectator is given temporary magical powers. He cuts the deck into four heaps. Then he deals cards from the top of each heap onto the other heaps. When he turns over the top card of each heap, he finds that he has located the four aces.

Method: Beforehand, place the four aces on top of the deck. Leave the deck in the case until the time of performance.

When presenting the trick, state that some people are lucky at cards. They seem to know where the good cards are. As you speak, remove the deck from the case and place it on the table. Have the spectator cut the deck in half, Figure 47. Keep track of which packet has the aces on top.

Tell the spectator to cut each packet in half. The result will be as shown in Figure 48. Keep track of where the aces are. In our example, they are on top of packet A.

Have the spectator pick up the packet at the opposite end of the row (packet D in our example). He deals three cards into position

D where the packet was originally. Then he deals one card onto A, B and C. He replaces packet D in its original position.

Next he picks up packet C. He deals three cards off the top of C into position C on the table where the packet was originally. He deals a card onto A, B and D. Then he replaces packet C in its original position.

Next he picks up packet B. He deals three cards off the top of B into position B on the table where the packet was originally. He deals a card onto A, C and D. Then he replaces packet B in its original position.

Finally, he picks up packet A. He deals three cards off the top of A into position A on the table where the packet was originally. He deals a card onto B, C and D. Then he replaces packet A in its original position.

Say, "Let's see how lucky you are." Turn up the top card of one packet, then the top card of another packet, then the top card of each of the remaining packets to reveal the four aces.

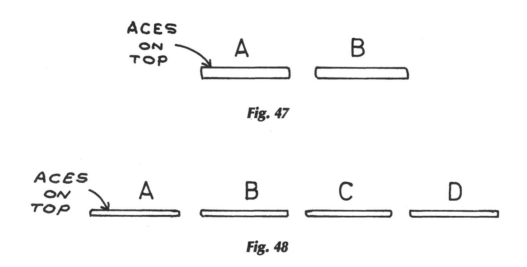

Fig. 47

Fig. 48

♠ Atomic Aces

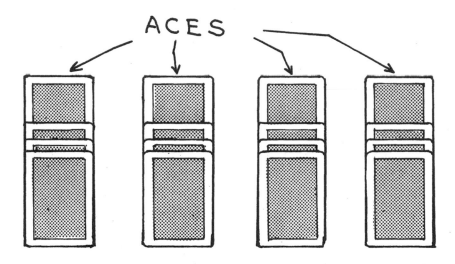

ACES

Fig. 49

This is a good routine to follow the previous trick, after the aces have been produced. Deal the aces face down into a row on the table. Then deal three cards on top of each ace, Figure 49.

Pick up the packet on the left and place it on the next packet. Place these on top of the next packet and these on top of the last packet. Hold the combined packet in the left hand.

Say, "The aces attract one another. Let me show you what I mean." Deal a row of four cards by dealing cards one at a time off the top of the packet on the table. Then deal the fifth card on top of the first. The situation is shown in Figure 50. Say, "Maybe it would be better if you dealt the cards."

Place the cards at A on top of B. Place these on top of C, and these on top of D. The packet in your hand is then placed on top of the five-card packet. Hand the complete packet to the spectator.

He deals the cards into four rows on the table, dealing from left to right, one card at a time, until all 16 cards have been dealt. There are now four heaps of four cards each.

Take the last card he dealt and turn it face up. It will be an ace. Say, "There's an ace buried in each packet. The old saying is that birds of a feather flock together. It works with aces as well."

Exchange the ace with the top card of the packet next to it. Pick up the packet on which you just placed the ace. Snap the fingers. Turn all four cards face up to reveal that the aces have gathered in this packet.

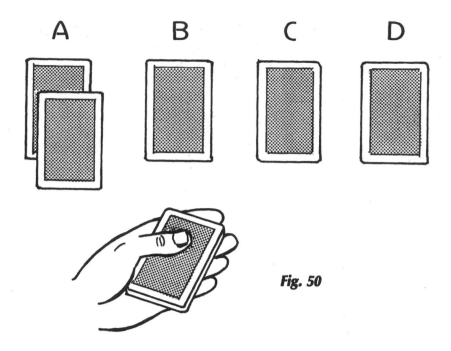

A   B   C   D

Fig. 50

Levitation ♥

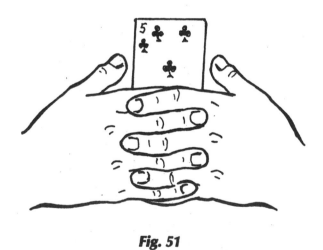

Fig. 51

A playing card mysteriously floats behind the hands as shown in Figure 51. There is no preparation. Any card may be used.

Method: The trick is done while seated at the table. Put a card face down on the table. Rub it back and forth. Say, "This causes the card to fall under a deep spell." Place the card so it overlaps the near edge of the table, Figure 52.

Bring the hands below the edge of the table so the hands cannot be seen by the spectator. Interlace the fingers as indicated in Figure 52.

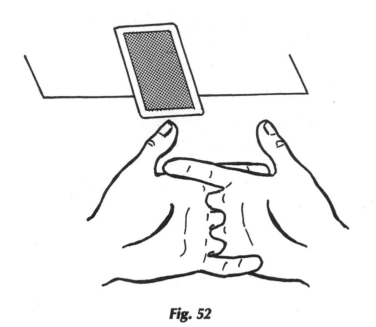

Fig. 52

Slide the right second (middle) finger out and put the right first (index) finger in its place. The situation is as shown in Figure 53.

Keeping the hands below the edge of the table, bring them to a position under the card. Use the thumbs to draw the card off the table and into the palm. Unknown to the audience, you are holding the card in place with the middle finger as shown in Figure 54.

Now bring the hands up into view. The audience sees the situation depicted in Figure 51. If the card is held firmly in place, you can shake the hands up and down to indicate that the card clings mysteriously to the hands.

Say, "Eventually the spell wears off." Quickly pull the hands apart. The card falls to the table.

Fig. 53

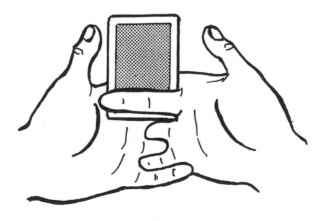

Fig. 54

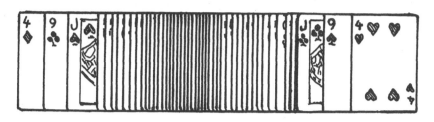

Fig. 55

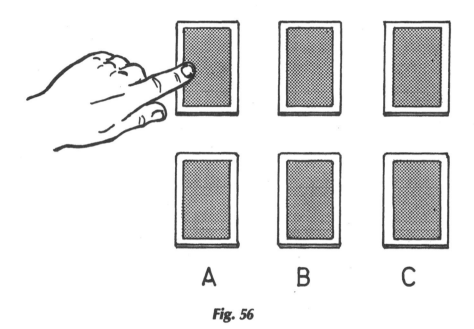

A　　　　B　　　　C

Fig. 56

In this impressive mystery the magician matches three cards chosen by the spectator.

Method: The ♦ 4, ♣ 9 and ♠ J are arranged on top of the deck. The ♣ J, ♠ 9 and ♥ 4 are arranged on the bottom of the deck. The setup is shown in Figure 55. This preparation is done secretly.

To present the trick, place the deck face down on the table. Ask the spectator to cut the deck into two heaps. Hand him the top half of the deck. Ask him to deal this packet into three heaps. He deals one card at a time from his left to his right. Wait until he has dealt all the cards in his packet.

Pick up the bottom half of the deck. Deal it into three heaps, dealing a card at a time from your left to your right.

Say, "The cards send signals that can sometimes be picked up with the fingers." Place your finger on top of each of the spectator's packets, Figure 56. Pick up your leftmost packet.

Place this packet out of sight behind the

back or under the table. Say, "Let's see if I can find some matching cards." When the packet is out of sight, take the top card and place it on the bottom. Then replace the packet on the table.

Perform the same actions with the other two packets you dealt. Then say, "If I'm lucky, I've been able to match your cards."

Turn over the spectator's packets. Say, "Your cards are a red four, a black nine and a black jack. Let's see how I did."

Turn over your packets to show you picked a red four, a black nine and a black jack, exactly matching his cards. The order of your cards may not match the order of his, but the values will always match.

♦ Fast Find

The magician removes three cards of the same value, shows them to the audience and mixes them into the deck. Then, by tossing the deck from hand to hand, he finds all four cards of the same value.

Method: Spread the deck between the hands so you can see the faces of the cards. Note the card second from the top of the deck. Whatever its value, remove the other three cards of the same value from the pack. In Figure 57

this card is an ace, so you would remove the other three aces from the deck.

On rare occasions you will find that the top two cards of the deck are the same value. In these cases, simply cut the deck, complete the cut and start again.

In our example three aces have been removed from the deck. Show the aces and place them in a face-down row on the table, Figure 58. Hold the deck face down. Deal a card off the top onto A, the next card onto B

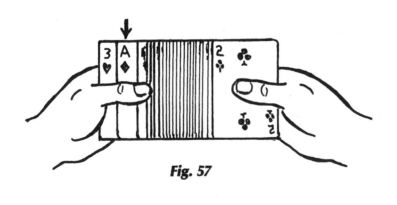

Fig. 57

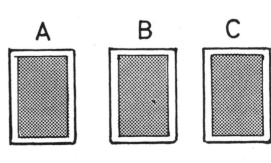

A   B   C

Fig. 58

and the next onto C. Pick up packet A and put it on top of the deck.

Deal the top card of the deck onto B and the next card onto C. Pick up packet B and place it on top of the deck.

Deal the top card of the deck onto C. Place packet C on top of the deck. Unknown to the audience, the aces are at positions 2, 4, 5 and 6 from the top.

Fig. 59

Say, "Let's mix the cards even further." Take the top card and bury it in the middle of the pack. Transfer the new top card to the bottom. Bury the next card in the middle. Transfer the next card to the bottom.

Hold the deck as in Figure 59 with the thumb on top, fingers on the bottom. Toss the deck from hand to hand. As you do, hold the top and bottom card in place, Figure 60. Note that in Figure 60 the deck is caught in the opposite hand so the thumb is on top and the fingers below.

Toss the deck onto the table, but retain the top and bottom card as shown in Figure 61.

Say, "We started with three aces, but we finish with all four aces." Turn over the cards in each hand to show you have caught the four aces.

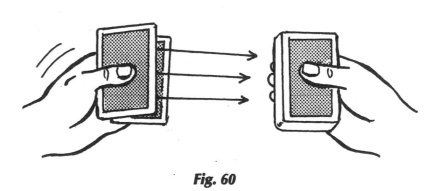

Fig. 60

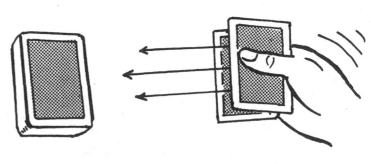

Fig. 61

♥ Hidden Diamonds

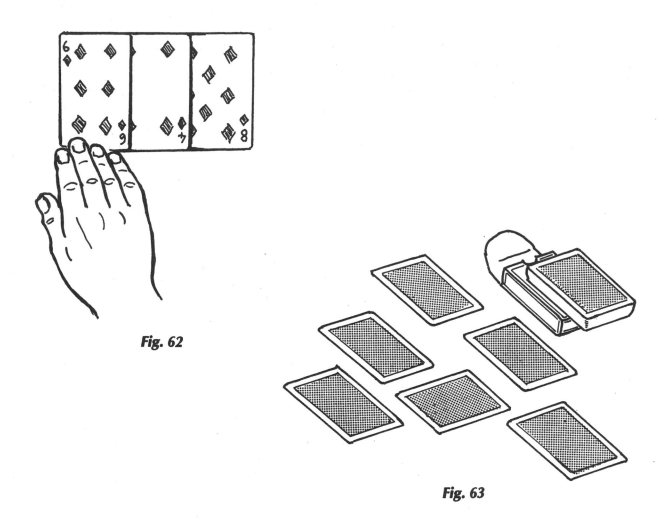

Fig. 62

Fig. 63

People enjoy a good story with a surprise ending. This is a card trick in which three boys seek diamonds. They find the treasure in an unexpected way.

Method: Twelve cards are stacked from the top down as follows: ♦ 8- ♦ 4- ♦ 6- ♥ J- ♦ J- ♠ J- ♥ Q- ♠ Q- ♦ Q- ♦ 7- ♦ 5- ♦ 3. Have this packet of cards in the pocket until the time of performance. Place the balance of the deck in the card case.

When ready to perform, remove the deck from the case and place it face down on the table. Remove the packet of 12 cards from the pocket and hold it face down in the hand. Say, "This is a story that uses nine cards."

Push over the top three cards. Place them face up in an overlapping row on the table, Figure 62. Say, "On the outskirts of a certain town there was a diamond mine with diamonds hidden somewhere. I don't have real diamonds with me, so I'll use these."

Scoop up the three cards, turn them face down and place them on the bottom of the packet.

Say, "Three boys went looking for the

diamonds." Push over the top three cards of the packet. Place them face up in an over-lapping row on the table to show the three jacks. Then scoop up the jacks, turn them face down and place them on the bottom of the packet.

Say, "The other players in this story are their three mothers, who worried about them." Take the three top cards of the packet and place them face up in an overlapping row on the table to show the three queens.

Scoop up the queens, turn them face down and place them on the bottom of the packet.

Place the packet on top of the deck. Then pick up the deck and hold it face down in the left hand. Say, "Of course the diamonds were scattered about." Deal the top three cards face down on the table. Leave space between the cards.

"One night the boys sneaked out looking for treasure." Deal the next three cards on the table in scattered fashion. "When their mothers found out, they got in a car and went looking for the boys." Deal off the next three cards. Without showing their faces, place the three cards in the card case.

"They drove around, got lost and ended up in a cave under the diamond mine." Place the card case on the table. Put the deck on top of it, Figure 63.

"The ladies were able to dig themselves out." This is the first surprise of the story. Turn up the top three cards of the deck to reveal the three queens.

"In the process they found a bushel of diamonds." Turn up all six cards on the table to show they are all diamonds.

"And where were the three boys? Asleep in the back seat of the car." Place the deck aside. Slide the three cards out of the card case and show the three jacks.